Helping Children See Jesus

ISBN: 978-1-64104-033-4

Human Suffering
Old Testament Volume 29: Job

Author: Arlene S Piepgrass
Illustrator: Vernon Henkel
Colorization: Olivia and Bethany Moy
Typesetting and Layout: Patricia Pope

© Bible Visuals International
PO Box 153, Akron, PA 17501-0153
Phone: (717) 859-1131
www.biblevisuals.org

All rights reserved. No part of this publication may be reproduced, stored in a retrieval system or transmitted in any form by any means, electronic, mechanical, photocopy, recording or otherwise, without the prior permission of the publisher, except as provided by USA copyright law.

RELATED ITEMS

To access related items (such as activities, memory verse posters and translated texts) please visit our web store at www.biblevisuals.org and enter 2029 at the top right of the web page. You may need to reduce the zoom setting to get the search box.

FREE TEXT DOWNLOAD

To obtain a FREE printable copy of the English teaching text (PDF format) under Product Format, please scroll down and select Extra–PDF Teacher Text Download. Then under Language select English before clicking the ADD TO CART button to place in your shopping cart. Other languages are available at an additional cost from the Language menu. When checking out, use coupon code XTACSV17 at checkout and click on Apply Coupon to receive the discount on the English text.

Blessed is the man that endureth temptation: for when he is tried, he shall receive the crown of life, which the Lord hath promised to those that love Him.

James 1:12

Lesson 1
APPROVED BY GOD

NOTE TO THE TEACHER

Probably the oldest book of the Bible is Job. There is no mention of the Jewish Law in Job. Therefore the book must have been written before God gave the Law. After his calamities recorded in Job, Chapter 1, Job lived 140 years. (See Job 42:16.) So he may have died at about age 200. This corresponds to the ages of men in the book of Genesis. Thus Job could have lived around the time of Abraham or Jacob.

The book of Job teaches us how one man suffered. From Job's experiences, we learn this: we are to trust God in suffering.

There are additional reasons for the suffering of Christian believers. For example: God sometimes sends suffering to chasten (discipline) His own (1 Corinthians 11:28-30). Suffering may be for our instruction (2 Corinthians 12:7-10). Suffering is part of the learning process. By it, a believer is prepared to share God's holiness (Hebrews 12:8-10). Suffering is proof of God's genuine love for His children (Hebrews12:6, 8). Suffering can be for a testimony to others (John 9:3). Suffering is the result of the battle between Satan and God (Job 1:1-2:13). Suffering comes because of the fall (Romans 8:20-23).

God's purpose always is to conform us to the image of His Son. His ways are right even though we may not understand them. (See Romans 8:28-29; Hebrews 12:11.) If we suffer with Christ, we shall also reign with Him (2 Timothy 2:12). Glorious truth!

On each of four posters, print one of Job's characteristics. (See Job 1:1-8.) Whenever one of these attributes is mentioned, display appropriate poster.

1. Job was BLAMELESS.
2. Job was UPRIGHT.
3. Job FEARED GOD.
4. Job TURNED FROM EVIL.

This lesson includes excellent material on each of these four subjects. You know your students. Therefore you will know how much to stress each character trait.

Scripture to be studied: Job 1:1-5, 8; verses cited in lesson

The *aim* of the lesson: To show that God approved of Job.

What your students should *know*: They can be acceptable to God.

What your students should *feel*: A desire to be approved by God.

What your students should *do*: Read the Bible and pray each day (2 Timothy 2:15; 1 Thessalonians 5:17-18).

Lesson outline (for the teacher's and students' notebooks):

1. Job's reputation in Uz (Job 1:3).
2. Job's family (Job 1:2, 4-5).
3. God's opinion of Job (Job 1:1, 8).
4. God's opinion of us (Verses cited in lesson).

The verse to be memorized:

Blessed is the man that endureth temptation: for when he is tried, he shall receive the crown of life, which the Lord hath promised to them that love Him. (James 1:12)

THE LESSON

Close your eyes for a moment. Think of someone you know who very much loves the Lord. Open your eyes. Now mention one word which describes that person. (Encourage response.)

Do you think God approves of the one you thought of? Why? Do you think God approves of you?

NOTE TO THE TEACHER

The Bible word "tempt" means to try, test, prove, or to lure to evil. In James 1:2, 12, "temptation" refers to being tested. A test is intended to prove the quality of one's character. The person who stands the test receives a "crown of life" (James 1:12). This is one of the rewards for the Christian.

God allowed Job to be tested. And he allows us to have testings. To persevere under testing is to be assured of eternal reward.

1. JOB'S REPUTATION IN US
Job 1:3

Long, long ago (maybe 4,000 years ago!) there lived a man named Job. He was "the greatest of all the men of the east" (Job 1:3). Do you want to know something about Job? Good! We shalt hurry to the city gate. This is where the men gather to carry on their business.

Show Illustration #1

Let's talk to that important-looking man. "What do you know about the man Job who lives here?"

"Job!" he exclaims. "He is the richest man in all the land. He has more sheep and camels than anyone!"

"Really? How many does he own?" we ask.

"He has 7,000 sheep and 3,000 camels," the man replies. "That is a lot of livestock! He hires many servants to care for them."

Another man adds, "That is not all Job owns. He also has 1,000 oxen and 500 female donkeys. He also owns more land than anyone else. Job is the wealthiest man I've ever known."

Let us total the number of animals Job owned. How many? (11,500!)

Now we turn to a younger man. "Job must be very proud since he is so rich."

"Oh, no! Not a bit," he says. "Job is kind and generous. He helps poor people and orphans (Job 29:12). He is sympathetic. He always comes to the aid of the blind and lame." (See Job 29:15.)

Right then the men stop talking. Looking up, we see a distinguished-looking man approaching. This is Job, the man loved and respected by everyone. All fix their eyes on him. They are eager to hear what Job will say. They seek his advice and follow it. (See Job 29:7-11, 21.)

2. JOB'S FAMILY
Job 1:2, 4-5

Soon we learn that Job has seven sons and three daughters– ten children, all grown. By listening, we understand that his children have their own families. Each son, on his birthday, has a party. He invites his brothers and sisters to his house. Sometimes the parties last several days. The family members love each other and enjoy being together.

We become aware of something else. Job is a praying father. He wants his children to live to please God.

Show Illustration #2

Job regularly offers sacrifices to God for his family. He prays, "O God, if my children have sinned, please forgive them." Job's sons and daughters are blessed to have a praying father. Besides praying for them, Job taught his family to worship God. This is what God wants fathers to do today. (See Ephesians 6:4.)

3. GOD'S OPINION OF JOB
Job 1:1, 8

We know what the people thought of Job. We understand he was a praying, caring father. And we have learned that he was very, very rich. But what did God think of Job? The Lord God's opinion is what really matters.

Show Illustration #3

Listen to what God, looking down from Heaven, said about Job. "There is no one like Job on earth. He is blameless and upright. He fears God and turns away from evil." (Show each poster.) These are four of Job's good qualities. What do they mean?

Job was blameless. (Display BLAMELESS poster.) That is, his greatest desire was to please God. Job had his faults. Like everyone else, Job was born a sinner. (See Psalm 14:1-3.) But God had taught Job to offer sacrifices for his sins. This Job did. And the Lord forgave him. So God spoke of Job as "blameless." Could He say that of you? He can, if you have truly accepted Christ as your sin-bearer. (See 1 Corinthians 1:8-9; Colossians 1:20-22; 1 Thessalonians 5:23.)

Job was upright. (Display UPRIGHT.) Upright means that Job was in right relationship to God–and to others. His conduct was right. If he made a promise, he kept it. He was dependable. He was honest. Everyone could trust Job. He was a good testimony for God to others. An upright person is a delight to the Lord. (See Proverbs 11:20.)

Job feared God. (Display poster.) Job respected God so much that he was afraid of displeasing God. He often offered sacrifices to the Lord. He asked God to forgive him for wrongs he had done. His greatest desire was to obey the Lord: God says those who fear Him are wise. (See Proverbs 9:10; Psalm 111:10.)

Job turned away from evil. (Display poster.) What is evil? (Let students respond, giving specific examples of sin. Read Proverbs 8:13.) God hates evil. Another word for "evil" is sin. The Bible says that those who love the Lord hate evil (Psalm 97:10). Because Job was blameless, upright and feared God, he turned away from evil. Job hated what God the Lord hated. Listen to some sins which God hates. (Read Proverbs 6:16-19 slowly, emphasizing each sin.) Job turned away from evil. Do you?

Would you like to have had Job for a friend? Would he have been trustworthy? Why? (Discuss. Point out that he would be considerate, helpful, honest, faithful.)

Job was approved by God. This is the best reputation anyone can have.

4. GOD'S OPINION OF US
Verses cited in lesson

As God looked down on Job, how did He describe him? (Display four posters. Let students review God's evaluation of Job.)

Show Illustration #4

The Lord God sees everyone in the world right now. (See Proverbs 5:21; 15:3.) This means He sees you. How would He describe you? Would He say you are blameless? Upright? Fearing God? Turning from evil? How can you be such a person?

BLAMELESS. (*Teacher:* Again display posters one at a time.) Have you never done one wrong thing? Are you perfect? Listen to what God says. (Read Romans 3:10-12 emphasizing the word "none.") Not one of us is righteous. This means you are not righteous. Nor am I. Then how can you be blameless in God's eyes? Listen carefully!

The Lord God loves you. Indeed, He loves you so much, He sent His Son to earth. His Son, the Lord Jesus, came to take the punishment for your sins. (Read Romans 5:8.) That punishment was death (1 Corinthians 15:3). You and I deserved to die because we are sinners (Romans 6:23a). But Christ, the perfect One, died in your place and mine. By dying, He took our sins on Himself. (See Isaiah 53:6; 1 Peter 2:24.)

Now, "If you . . . confess with your mouth the Lord Jesus, and . . . believe in your heart that God . . . raised Him from the dead, you shall be saved" (Romans 10:9). "Believe on the Lord Jesus Christ, and you shall be saved . . ." (Acts 16:31). Have you believed in the Lord Jesus? (John 3:16.) Do you believe you are a sinner? Do you understand the awfulness of sin? Sinners will be separated from God forever and ever. (See Romans 6:23; Revelation 20:15.) Do you believe the Lord Jesus died for your sins? Will you place your trust in Him to save you? If you truly do this, God will forgive your sins. He will say you are no longer guilty. (See Romans 4:5, 8.) You are BLAMELESS in God's eyes. (See Colossians 1:21-22; Jude 24.)

UPRIGHT. Are you in right relationship with God? If you have truly received Christ, He lives in your heart. (See Galatians 2:20.) Does your conduct prove that the Lord Jesus is living in you? God approves UPRIGHT conduct. (See Colossians 3:5-4:6; Proverbs 1:8; Ephesians 6:1-3; Romans 13:9; 14:19; 1 Corinthians 13:5. Teacher: Choose admonitions appropriate for the needs of your group.)

The Lord warns us against making friends of those who do wrong. (See Proverbs 1:10-15.) Why do you think God says this? (We often do what our friends do.) It is important for us to be UPRIGHT–and to choose upright friends. (See Proverbs 13:20; 1 Corinthians 5:9-11.)

Does it sound easy to be upright? (No.) You cannot be UPRIGHT without God's help. And He is willing to help you do right. Will you ask Him to do so? (See Proverbs 15:8.)

FEAR GOD. This means we want to please God most of all. (Read Proverbs 23:26.) How can we please Him? By allowing Him to control our lives. Fearing God does not mean we are afraid of Him. Rather, we are fearful of displeasing Him.

TURN AWAY FROM EVIL. (Ask students to mention sinful habits, attitudes and activities.) The Lord says we are to turn from evil. We are not even to think about evil! (See 1 Corinthians 13:5.) We must ask God to help us.

Jabez (a man mentioned in the Old Testament) prayed: "O God . . . bless me. Help me in my work. Please be with me in all I do . . . And keep me from all evil . . ." (See 1 Chronicles 4:10.) And God gave Jabez what he asked. The Lord will answer you, too, if you pray as Jabez did.

Show Illustration #4

Job was approved by God. Are you? Would you like to have His approval? To be approved by the Lord, you must study and obey the Bible. (Read 2 Timothy 2:15.) Obeying God's Word may seem hard. But it will be much, much harder if you disobey it!

If you have trusted in Christ, God's Holy Spirit lives within you. (See 1 Corinthians 3:16; 6:19-20.) He is willing to help you to please the Lord. (See Galatians 5:16, 22-23.) Starting today, will you read your Bible, obey it and pray?

Will you do so every day? Ask God for the help you need to be approved by Him.

Lesson 2
SATAN, JOB'S ENEMY

NOTE TO THE TEACHER

Satan wants everyone to disobey the Lord and rebel against Him. Whenever we doubt or defy God, Satan wins the victory. Help your students to understand this.

The Lord commands: "Submit yourselves . . . to God. Resist the devil and he will flee from you. Draw close to God and He will draw close to you" (James 4:7-8a). To submit to God, we willingly put ourselves under His control. We must decide whether we will be on God's side or Satan's. When we are on God's side, we must firmly refuse to obey Satan. And we are continually to come near to God. As we do, the Lord comes near to us.

We "come near to God" by carefully studying and obeying His Word. Then He enables us to say "no" to Satan.

For every believer, daily, faithful Bible reading and prayer are imperative!

Use the four posters which you prepared for Lesson #1.

Are you teaching children or new-born Christians? If so, have students enact a short skit reviewing the previous lesson.

Scripture to be studied: Job 1:6-2:10; Ezekiel 28:11-19; Isaiah 14:12-14

The *aim* of the lesson: To show that God's enemy, Satan, is our enemy also.

What your students should *know*: That Satan wants believers to doubt God and rebel against Him.

What your students should *feel*: A desire to resist the devil so he will flee from them.

What your students should *do*: Draw near to God by reading the Bible and praying.

Lesson outline (for the teacher's and students' notebooks):
1. Who is Satan? (Ezekiel 28:11-19; Isaiah 14:12-14).
2. Satan accuses Job (Job 1:6-19)
3. Job's response (Job 1:20-2:10).
4. Satan, our accuser (Revelation 12:10; 1 Peter 5:8).

The verse to be memorized:

Blessed is the man that endureth temptation: for when he is tried, he shall receive the crown of life, which the Lord hath promised to them that love Him. (James 1:12)

THE LESSON

Job was a person we would like to have had as a friend. Why? (Teacher: Show posters. He was blameless and upright. He feared God and turned from evil.) Job was a good man. So good, that even the Lord God spoke well of him. But there was someone who was ready to tempt Job. Who do you think this could be? (Allow suggestions.) Satan was eager to tempt Job. Why? Listen carefully!

1. WHO IS SATAN?
Ezekiel 28:11-19; Isaiah 14:12-14

Satan is the enemy of God. But this was not always so. God created Satan even before He created Adam and Eve. At first, Satan's name was Lucifer, meaning "day-star." Of all the angels God created, Satan was the most beautiful.

God chose Lucifer to rule over the other angels. The Bible says Satan was created perfect. (See Ezekiel 28:12, 15.) He thought no wrong. He did no wrong. He worshiped Almighty God, the holy, glorious, most powerful One.

But one day something dreadful happened. Lucifer had a wicked thought. He said to himself, "One as beautiful and wise as I, should be worshiped. I should not have to worship Another. I want to be like God, the highest of all. I want to have His majesty and power."

Lucifer was no longer satisfied simply to rule over other angels. He wanted the angels to worship him as they worshiped God. Lucifer wanted to take the place of Almighty God. Think of that!

So Lucifer planned what he would do. He said, "I shall go into the highest Heaven. I shall have my throne above the stars of God. I shall rule above the clouds. I shall be like God." (See Isaiah 14:12-14.) Lucifer wanted to be completely independent of God. That was sin–the very first sin.

God who is holy, could not permit sin (rebellion) in Heaven. So He punished Lucifer by taking his high position from him.

Show Illustration #5

God cast Lucifer out of Heaven. No longer could he serve the Lord God. Because he had sinned, Lucifer's beautiful name was changed to Satan– the devil. "Satan" means adversary (the enemy). "The devil" means accuser.

Now Satan hated God! Never again would he obey and serve the Lord. He would rule for himself. Satan hated all of God's good plans and determined to spoil them. He had ideas of his own. He would scheme against the Lord.

2. SATAN ACCUSES JOB
Job 1:6-19

According to their custom, the angels gathered before God in Heaven. They gave good reports of their service for Him. Satan went along with them. He had nothing good to report. But he had to give an account of his activities.

God asked, "Satan, where have you come from?"

"I've been going back and forth over the earth," replied Satan.

The Lord said, "Have you observed my servant, Job? There is no one like him on earth. He is blameless and upright. (Show posters.) He fears Me and turns away from evil."

"Of course he does right," Satan answered, with a sneer. "You take good care of him. Look how rich You have made him! No wonder he worships You. You protect him, his family and everything he owns. But take away his wealth. Then You will see how good he is! He will no longer worship You. Instead, he will curse You to Your face."

Job worshiped God because he loved Him. The Lord knew this. So He did not argue with the devil, but simply said, "Satan, you may do whatever you like with what Job has. But you may not harm his body."

The Lord of Heaven and earth permitted Satan to test Job.

Satan left the presence of the Lord filled with pride. "I'll show God how good Job is!" he said. "It won't be long before he curses God!"

Show Illustration #6

Shortly thereafter, a terrified messenger ran to Job at his home. "We were working in the fields with the oxen," he gasped. "Suddenly our enemies, the Sabeans, attacked us. They took all your oxen and donkeys, then killed all your servants. I'm the only one who escaped!"

Speechless, Job thought, I must rescue my animals!

Before he could make plans, another servant came running. Panting, he shouted, "Lightning struck from Heaven and all your sheep were destroyed! All the servants caring for them were killed, too. I am the only one who escaped."

Immediately, a third servant dashed in. "Oh, master Job!" he cried. "Something dreadful has happened. Our enemies, the Chaldeans, made a surprise attack on us. They stole all your camels and killed all the servants. I am the only one who escaped."

In almost no time, Job had lost all his animals. And his servants lay dead. He, the very rich man, now had nothing.

Job's mind was awhirl when a fourth messenger darted inside. "Job, I have dreadful news!" The messenger struggled for breath. "Your sons and daughters were feasting together. Suddenly a blast of wind hit the house. The building collapsed and all your sons and daughters are dead. I'm the only one who escaped."

Satan, thinking ugly thoughts, watched to see what Job would do. To himself he said, "Now Job is poor. And his sons and daughters are dead. Soon he'll curse God. Then we shall see how blameless and upright he is!"

3. JOB'S RESPONSE
Job 1:20-2:10

Had you been in Job's place, what would you have done? (Discuss.) Most people would cry, "O God! Why did You do this to me?" Some would ask, "What have I done to deserve this?" Others would say, "I am angry with God! I know He does not care about me."

This is what Satan was waiting to hear Job say. Then he could return to God saying, "I told You so! Job obeyed You only because You were good to him. I knew he really didn't love You."

Satan waited and waited.

Job was broken-hearted. But listen to what he did. (Read Job 1:20-22.) Job, in great sadness, tore his robe and shaved his head.

Show Illustration #7

Then Job worshiped the Lord. He could not understand why his children and everything else had been destroyed.

But he looked to God. "Dear Lord," he prayed, "You gave me all I had. Now You have taken away everything. You have the right to do this. Blessed be Your name."

Job had trusted the Lord when everything went well. He was used to worshiping God. Now with all his troubles, he turned to the Lord. He neither sinned nor cursed God. So Satan was defeated.

But the devil never gives up easily. Again he reported to God. The Lord asked him, "Have you observed My servant Job? He is the finest man on the earth. He is blameless and upright. He fears Me and turns away from evil. I have allowed you to test him. Now you know that Job has kept his faith in Me."

Satan answered, "Skin for skin. Touch his body and he'll curse You. Let me make him sick. Then see if he will worship You."

"Job will not rebel against Me, Satan," God replied. "You may test him to prove that. But you may not take his life."

Satan wasted no time. He left the presence of the Lord. And immediately he caused Job to have boils (sores) all over his body. Horrible, painful sores. Boils from the soles of his feet to the top of his head. Poor, miserable Job! He could not eat. He could not sleep. He did not even stay in his home. Instead, he sat on an ash heap outside the city. Not long before, Job sat at the city gate. There he was one of the respected leaders of the city. Now he was sitting where beggars sit. He scraped his painful boils with a piece of broken pottery. Never had he suffered like this.

Satan waited, thinking, Surely now Job will curse God. Instead, Job suffered silently.

Satan did not give up. This time he prompted Job's wife to discourage him. She asked, "Job, what good is your faith in God? Look what He has done to you. Curse Him and die."

This was exactly what Satan wanted to hear! But what a blow it must have been to Job! His children were dead. He had only his wife to encourage him. But she was no comfort at all.

Do you think Job agreed with his wife and cursed God? Listen to his answer. "My wife, you are talking foolishly like the heathen women. Shall we receive only good from God? Shall we never receive anything unpleasant from His hand? You were happy when everything was going well. Why are you now angry at the Lord? He is always the same."

Again, Satan was defeated. He'd tried every possible way to make Job curse God. But in all this, Job did not sin with his lips.

Satan was not finished, as we shall learn in our next lesson. Job continued suffering outside the city on the ash heap. Job could not understand why all this was happening to him. But he did not blame God. Job continually trusted and worshiped the Lord God of Heaven.

4. SATAN, OUR ACCUSER
Revelation 12:10; 1 Peter 5:8

Satan is the enemy of God. He was Job's enemy. And he is our enemy also. More than anything else, Satan wants everyone to rebel against God. He does not want anyone to place their trust in God's Son. (See 2 Corinthians 4:3-4.) Those who believe in the Lord Jesus, will be forever with God in Heaven. (See John 3:16, 36.) Satan knows this. He knows, too, that he will go to the lake of fire (hell) forever. (See Revelation 20:10, 15.) And he wants all people everywhere to be with him there. Everyone who rebels against God and rejects Christ as Saviour, will be there. Listen to what the Lord Jesus will say some day. ". . . Depart from Me, you who are cursed, into everlasting fire, prepared for the devil and his angels" (Matthew 25:41).

Have you trusted God and believed in His Son? Is the Lord Jesus Christ your Saviour?

Job trusted God. He was God's loyal, faithful servant. Yet Satan tried to make Job rebel against God.

If you belong to the Lord, Satan will work on you. He will try to get you to rebel against the Lord. For "the devil, like a roaring lion, walks about, seeking whom he may devour" (1 Peter 5:8). How does Satan "devour" the believer in Christ? He seizes you with many testings, many temptations. Whenever you yield to Satan, your life becomes useless for God.

Satan may tempt you to be angry with God. He may tempt you to doubt God's goodness. He will often tempt you not to read the Bible or pray. He sometimes may tempt you not to go to church or Sunday school. So the devil "devours" you. And you are of no use to God.

How can you avoid being devoured by Satan? (Teacher Read James 4:7-8a slowly and emphatically.) You must submit yourself to God, allowing Him to control you. You have to resist the devil–say "NO!" to him. Every time you are tempted to do wrong, say, "No, Satan!" You must choose to do right. When you refuse to obey Satan, he will flee from you. Soon, however, he will come with another temptation. Again, refuse to follow him. Say "NO!"

Show Illustration #8

Continually you must come near to God. You do this by reading His Word, the Bible. When you come near to God, He comes near to you. He speaks to you through His Word. You speak to Him in prayer. Ask Him to help you to obey His Word. Our enemy, Satan, is strong. But the Lord is much stronger. (See 1 John 4:4.) He is the only One who can make you strong. If you will resist the devil, he will flee from you. Pray each day for God's help.

God promises you will not be tested beyond what you can stand. He Himself will make a way out. Thus you will be able to stand up under the testing. (See 1 Corinthians 10:13.)

Remember! The Christian believer who endures testings, will receive the crown of life. The Lord has promised this to those who love Him. (See James 1:12.)

Lesson 3
JOB'S FRIENDS
(Can be taught in two parts)

NOTE TO THE TEACHER

To prepare, read Eliphaz's, Bildad's and Zophar's speeches, and Job's answers to each. Summarize the thoughts in each conversation. List these in your notebook. For simplicity, we have grouped each man's several speeches into one speech each.

Make four posters. On each, place an outline figure of a man. Add the name of one of each of Job's four friends: Eliphaz, Bildad, Zophar, Elihu.

You may wish to spend two class periods on this material. If so, use lesson points #1 and #2 with illustrations in the first session. Begin the second lesson by reviewing Job's friends' accusations and his replies. Have students tell their experiences in helping suffering friends.

True friends are a gift from God. Help your students understand that friends can hurt or help. Christian friends who know God's Word are encouragers in difficult times. Sometimes they must hurt us for our good. (See Proverbs 27:6a.) Friends have a great influence on us. So it is important to choose the right kinds of friends.

Scripture to be studied: Job 2:11-42:17

The *aim* of the lesson: To show that Job's friends failed him but God did not.

What your students should *know*: That we cannot always rely on the advice of friends.

What your students should *feel*: A desire to be wise and Godlike in helping suffering friends. (See Proverbs 17:17.)

What your students should *do*: Reach out to a friend who is suffering.

Lesson outline (for the teacher's and students' notebooks):

1. Job's friends fail to comfort him
   a. Eliphaz (The most sympathetic of Job's friends) Speech #1 (Job 4:1-5:27); Speech #2 (15:1-35); Speech #3 (22:1-30).
   b. Bildad (Less sensitive than Eliphaz) Speech #1 (Job 8:1-22); Speech #2 (18:1-21); Speech #3 (25:1-6).
   c. Zophar (The most blunt and harsh of the three. He considered himself to be the final authority.) Speech #1 (Job 11:1-20)2; Speech #2 (20: 1-29).
2. Job replies to his friends
   a. To Eliphaz's first speech (Job 6:1-7:21); second speech (16:1-17:16); third speech (23:1-24:25).
   b. To Bildad's first speech (Job 9:1-10:22); Second speech (19:1-29); third speech (26:1-14).
   c. To Zophar's first speech (Job 12:1-14:22; second speech (21:1-34).
   d. To all three friends (Job 27:1-31:40).
3. Elihu's counsel (Job 32:1-37:24).
4. God's response to Job and his friends (Job 38:1-42:9).

The verse to be memorized:

Blessed is the man that endureth temptation: for when he is tried, he shall receive the crown of life, which the Lord hath promised to them that love Him. (James 1:12)

THE LESSON

I feel sorry for Job. Do you? He had no one to comfort him. His whole body ached. His children would have cheered him but they were dead. How he missed them! Job's wife was so angry that she was no encouragement whatsoever. She had said, "Job, curse God and die!" (Job 2:9). Like Job, she was heartbroken. Job's ten children–and hers!–were dead. Only a few days before they were a wealthy family. Now they were poor. Job had been strong and healthy. Now he was sick and miserable. No wonder his wife wanted him to curse God and die. She was wrong, of course. But before criticizing her, check on yourself. How would you act if everything was taken from you?

Job needed a friend to comfort him. What is a friend? (Discuss.) The Bible says a friend is one who loves you. (See Proverbs 17:17.) A real friend understands you. A true friend accepts you as you are. A loyal friend laughs with you when you are happy. When you are sad, your friend is sad with you. Job needed a helpful, understanding friend.

1. JOB'S FRIENDS FAIL TO COMFORT HIM

Three of Job's friends heard what had happened to him. Their names were Eliphaz, Bildad and Zophar. (Show appropriate posters as you name each one.) "We must go and comfort Job," they decided. So off they went outside the city gates.

At first they did not recognize him. Coming closer, when they realized it was Job, they cried loudly. They tore their robes and threw dust over their heads.

Show Illustration #9

Job, the "greatest man in the east," was sitting on heaped-up ashes. I heard Job was sick," one whispered. "But I did not realize it was this bad!"

The three men wailed. They rubbed dirt on their heads. They wanted Job to know they felt sorry for him. But they did not speak to him.

One murmured, "What could he have done to deserve such misery?"

The three sat down on the ground near Job. For seven days and seven nights they sat with him. But they never said a word to him. They saw he was in dreadful pain. Finally Job cried, "I wish I'd never been born! I wish I'd died when I was a baby. Life has no meaning." (See Job 3:1-11.)

Job wondered why God had let him be born. But he did NOT curse God. Satan wanted Job to believe that: (1) His troubles came from God and (2) God sent the troubles because He did not love Job.

Job's friends should have encouraged him. They should have comforted him. Instead, listen to what they said.

Eliphaz spoke first. (Show poster with ELIPHAZ's name.) "Job, you have been a good man. You have helped many others who had problems. But now when you have trouble, you are heart-broken. (See Job 4:2-5.) I want to tell you this, Job. I have never seen an innocent man suffer. Suffering is always God's judgment for sin. (See Job 4:7-9.) I do not know what wrong you have done, Job. But surely you have sinned. That is why you have such severe suffering. Job, if I were in your place, I would seek God. I would ask Him why such suffering had come to me. Turn to God, Job. Confess your sins to Him!" (See Job 5:8.)

Job had not forgotten God. Can you recall what he said when his troubles began? He said, "The Lord gave. The Lord has taken away. Blessed be the name of the Lord" (Job 1:21). (Read also Job 2:10.)

Eliphaz continued. "Do you think you are suffering because you have been good? Not at all. It is because of your wickedness! Your sins are endless.' (See Job 22:4-5.) You were kind to the rich. But you must have refused to help the poor."

That was a lie. Do you remember Job's reputation? Do you remember what the people said about him? (Read Job 29:12-15.)

"You refused to help widows and orphans," Eliphaz added. This, too, was not true. (See Job 29:13.) "Job, admit you are wrong and you will have peace. Make things right in your life. Look up to God. He will hear you. He will help you." (See Job 22:21-30.)

Would you like to have Eliphaz for a friend? Would he help and encourage you? How would he make you feel? (Encourage discussion.)

Now Bildad had something to say. (Hold up BILDAD poster.) "Job, your children must have done something terribly wrong. That surely is the reason they all died." (See Job 8:3-6.)

How those words hurt Job! Do you recall what Job did regularly for his children? (Job was a praying father. He continually offered sacrifices to God for them. He wanted his children to be forgiven of their sins. This was in obedience to God's command. See Job 1:5.)

Bildad continued, "Job, God is just. He does not send evil to good people. To those who are good, God gives happiness and laughing. (See Job 8:20-21.) If you were a good man, Job, God would bless you. But He has taken everything from you because you are wicked." (See Job 18:5.)

Bildad judged Job harshly. But he did not know the facts. This is a good lesson for us. (Read Matthew 7:1.) Do you criticize others quickly? Do you always know all the facts?

Was Bildad a help to Job? No! Job did not need to be criticized. He needed someone to comfort him.

Zophar spoke next. (Display ZOPHAR poster.)

"Job, you claim to be pure in the eyes of God. I wish God would speak and tell you what He thinks! If only He would make you see yourself as you really are. He knows everything you have done. Listen to me! God is doubtless punishing you much less than you deserve!" (See Job 11:4-6.)

Was Zophar an encourager? Not at all.

Zophar continued. "Before you turn to God, get rid of your sins. Only then can you approach God without fear." (See Job 11:13-16.) Zophar (like Bildad) did not know the facts. He was falsely accusing Job.

2. JOB REPLIES TO HIS FRIENDS

Put yourself in Job's place. What would you say to Eliphaz, Bildad and Zophar? (Encourage discussion.) Listen as Job answers his friends.

"What miserable comforters you are!" Job exclaimed. (See Job 16:2.) "You think you are wise. Well, I am as wise as you. (See Job 12:2-3.) If you needed comfort, I would try to encourage you. (See Job 16:5.) How long are you going to trouble me? You are trying to break me with your long speeches. Ten times you have called me a sinner. You should be ashamed to deal so harshly with me. I am not guilty. You cannot prove what you have said." (See Job 19:1-5; 13:7-12.)

Remember! Job did not understand why such suffering had come to him. He knew nothing of the conversation between God and Satan.

Show Illustration #10

"I wish I could die!" Job wailed. (See Job 14:13.) "My life is short and full of tragedy (Job 9:25). I am tired of living (Job 10:1). Here I sit on a heap of ashes. My eyes are red from weeping. My friends mock me (Job 16:15-20). I tell you, I am innocent!" (Read of Job's despair in Job 19:13-20.)

"Oh pity me, my friends," Job cried. "God has struck me with His hand."

Satan was watching. He thought, I am glad no one is comforting Job. It is good to see how miserable he is. Now Job will curse God, just as I said.

Do you think Job cursed God? (Would you?)

Listen to what Job told his friends. "God is wise and powerful. (See Job 12:13.) He has created the heavens, the stars and the earth. (Job 9:8-9; 26:7.) He causes earthquakes and controls the storms. (Job 9:6, 8; 12:15.) It is God who gives life to every living thing (Job 12:10). He reigns over the leaders of nations. Sometimes He makes them strong and wise. Or He may weaken them and cause them to fall. He may make a nation great and later destroy it" (Job 12:17-25).

Job knew that the Lord is always in command of everything. Job had more to say. "Oh, I wish I knew where to find God. I could tell Him my troubles. He would listen to me. He would sympathize with me. He would be honest with me. (See Job 23:3-7.) I would ask Him why He is making me suffer. Why is He destroying me? Why did He let me be born? Was it so He could make me miserable?" (See Job 10:1-22.)

Remember: Job didn't have the Bible as we do. God's Word was not yet written. So he couldn't turn to it for comfort.

Job could not understand the troubles which had come to him. He said, "God is angry with me. He has taken away my children. He has made me sick. My whole body hurts! The Lord has caused my friends to laugh and mock me. (See Job 16:6-16.) I wish I could die!" (See Job 14:13.)

Hearing Job, Satan was happy. He thought, Now that things are bad enough, Job will curse God. I cannot wait to hear him.

But listen! Job said, "God may kill me. Still I shall hope in Him (Job 13:15). I do not understand what He is doing to me. But He knows all about me. He will do to me what He has planned." (See Job 23:10, 14.)

(*Teacher:* Slowly read Job 19:25-27 to your students. Or, if they have Bibles, let them read in unison.)

What a glorious hope Job had! He knew that after death he would see God. Are you certain you will go to Heaven after you die? Do you know you will see the Lord face to face? How can you know? (Explain the way of salvation. See page 8.)

Job said, "I wish I had a mediator. He would go between God and me." (Teacher: Explain that a mediator listens to both sides of an argument. Then he reconciles the two.)

Job continued, "A mediator would listen to me and defend me. He would give me God's answers to my questions. I cannot plead my own case. I am a mere man. The Lord God is mighty and great. I cannot stand alone before Him." (See Job 9:32-33.)

Job could not go to God through the Lord Jesus. Why? Because Christ had not yet come to earth to die for sinners. Today, the Lord Jesus Christ is our Mediator (1 Timothy 2:5-6). We, too, are merely people. But when Christ is our Saviour, we approach God through Him. (See Hebrews 4:15-16.)

Job cried, "Why are You treating me like this, dear Lord? Why are You angry with me? I am righteous. (See Job 32:1; 34:5.) I am innocent (Job 33:9). Why are You making me suffer? Why? Why? Why?"

Job could not understand God's purposes. He doubted God's love. But he never cursed God. (*Teacher:* Encourage students to tell their recent experiences in comforting suffering friends.)

3. ELIHU'S COUNSEL
Job 32:1-37:24

Through all these long speeches, a younger man was listening. His name was Elihu. (Display ELIHU poster.) He waited politely for the older men to finish.

He began: "Eliphaz, Bildad, Zophar, you are wrong. You have judged Job and condemned him. But you have not given him an answer. You have been no help." (See Job 32:2-10.)

Show Illustration #11

Turning to Job, Elihu continued. "You are wrong too, Job. You are trying to prove that God is wrong. You insist you are good and do not deserve to suffer. (See Job 33:1-11.)

"You, Job, want an explanation from the Lord. I want to be the mediator you wished for. I have been listening to you. Now let me give you God's message." Elihu spoke sympathetically.

"The Lord God is greater than you. You know that, don't you, Job?" asked Elihu (Job 33:12).

Job nodded in agreement.

Elihu continued, "Do you have the right to demand an explanation for God's actions? (See Job 33:13.) The Lord knows what He is doing. He has a purpose for everything He brings into our lives. Remember: God never does wrong

(Job 34:12). Simply submit to Him. Trust Him. Believe that He loves you. Suffering is not always punishment. Sometimes God uses suffering to cause people to trust Him more. He may use your suffering to make you stronger in character." (See Job 36:10-12, 16.)

Now Elihu asked some questions. "Job, do you know how God makes lightning? Do you know how He hangs clouds in the sky?"

Job could not answer these questions.

Elihu continued, "What God does is beyond our understanding. He makes snow fall on the earth. He makes rain pour down on man and animals. Do you understand how He does this, Job?" Again Job remained silent. He could not answer. (See Job 37:3-8, 15-16.)

"You know these things happen," Elihu said. "But you cannot explain them. So you cannot understand why God has given you these problems. He may never explain His reason to you. But you can be certain He has a purpose. And that purpose is for your good. He will never forsake you, Job. Believe Him and trust Him." (Job 37:23-24.)

Would you like to have a friend like Elihu? I would. He did not condemn Job, nor ridicule him. He turned Job's thoughts to God. Let us learn this lesson from Elihu.

4. GOD'S RESPONSE TO JOB AND HIS FRIENDS
Job 38:1-42:9

Often Job had wished the Lord would speak to him. He wanted God to give him answers.

Today the Lord speaks to us through the Bible. But Job did not have the Bible. So the Lord God Himself spoke directly to Job:

Show Illustration #12

"You have asked many questions, Job. Now I have some questions for you. Where were you when I created the earth? What keeps the earth in space? Do you know who created the oceans, Job? Who said to the waves, 'You may come so far; no farther'? (**Teacher:** Are your students familiar with the ocean? If so, emphasize the marvel of the boundary of the sea.)

"Job, can you make the sun rise in the morning? Do you know where night-time darkness comes from? Can you control the seasons? Are you able to make it rain? Can you count the stars?"

Job did not say a word. He had no answers.

God had more questions. "Job, who feeds the birds? Who made some animals wild so you cannot tame them? Who gives strength to the horse? Can you command the eagle to build his nest? Can you catch a crocodile and make him serve you? Job, can you do any of these?"

Job had no answer.

The Lord had another question. "Do you want to continue to argue with Me, the Almighty?"

"Oh no, Lord God!" Job cried. "I am nothing. I cover my mouth with my hand. I have said too much already. Almighty God, You are majestic. You are good. You are powerful. I have sinned. I questioned Your justice. I doubted Your love. I did not trust You. I thought You did not know what You were doing."

Catching his breath, Job prayed, "O Lord God, please forgive me. Now I understand that You know all things. I know You love me. I know You always do what is best for me."

Did God explain to Job the reason for his suffering? We do not know. But this we know: Job realized that God is always in control. He knew that what the Lord allowed is best. He no longer asked "Why?" He believed God works for the good of those who love Him. (See Romans 8:28.)

We know, too, that God forgave Job.

What about Eliphaz, Bildad and Zophar? The Lord scolded them, saying, "I am angry with you! You have not told the truth about Me. You said suffering is always My punishment for sin. This is not true. You accused Job falsely. You are the ones who have sinned. You must offer sacrifices to Me for your sins. Ask Job to pray for you. I shall hear his prayer and forgive you."

Job's three friends solemnly obeyed the Lord. And He forgave them.

Who was defeated? *(Satan)* Who was exalted? *(The Lord God)* What do you think happened to Job? How did he feel? What did he say? We shall learn the answers to these questions in our next lesson.

Which of the four men was an example of a good friend? *(Elihu)* Why? *(He did not accuse Job. He caused Job to look to God rather than his problems.)*

Do you have a friend who is suffering greatly? Have you been like Job's three unkind friends? Will you ask God to make you helpful like Elihu? What can you do this week to encourage a suffering friend? (Discuss.)

Lesson 4
LESSONS LEARNED FROM JOB

Scripture to be studied: Job 42:10-17; verses cited in lesson

The *aim* of the lesson: To show what Job teaches about God and about suffering.

What your students should *know*: That suffering is not necessarily punishment for sin.

What your students should *feel*: Thankfulness that God the Father loves us.

What your students should *do*: Acknowledge God's control in every part of their lives. This week, reach out as a friend to someone in need.

Lesson outline (for the teacher's and students' notebooks):
1. Job's new family (Job 42:10-17).
2. Job's new understanding about God
3. Job's new understanding about suffering
4. Lessons learned from Job

The verse to be memorized:

Blessed is the man that endureth temptation: for when he is tried, he shall receive the crown of life, which the Lord hath promised to them that love Him. (James 1:12)

NOTE TO THE TEACHER

Apply the truths of Job to the lives of your students. This is imperative!

Suffering in the lives of Christians:
1. **Is not necessarily punishment for sin–though it can be. (See Hebrews 12:6.)**
2. **Sometimes suffering is a test of faith to strengthen believers. Such suffering makes believers more useful to God. (See Psalm 66:10; James 1:2-3.) This truth should erase discouragement from those who are suffering. It should make observers less critical of those who are suffering.**

See additional reasons for suffering under the Notes to the Teacher section for Lesson #1.

THE LESSON

Have you ever had difficulties which eventually turned out good? (Encourage student discussion.) Job certainly had some bad experiences. Today we shall learn how everything turned out for Job. Listen carefully!

1. JOB'S NEW FAMILY
Job 42:10-17

How many children did Job have before his suffering? *(Ten–seven sons and three daughters)* What did the people in his land say about Job before his testing? (Review his reputation from Lesson #1. Show Illustration #1.) What had God told Satan about Job? *(He was blameless, upright, he feared God and turned from evil. Show four posters.)*

After the devil attacked Job, Job was broken-hearted. His body was dreadfully painful. His friends falsely accused him. It seemed as if the whole world was against him.

But that was not true. Who was not against him? *(The Lord)* The Bible records a wonderful promise for God's own. It is this: He will never allow more testings than the Christian can stand. (See 1 Corinthians 10:13.)

So God said to Satan, "That is enough. You have tested Job severely. You have not been able to make him curse Me. My servant Job is blameless and upright. He fears Me. He turns away from evil. See, Satan? Job truly loves Me. He does not love Me for what I give him. Now go your way, Satan. Do not trouble Job anymore."

Satan fled in defeat. Always he must obey the Lord God.

Show Illustration #13

The Lord healed Job's body. Then his family and friends gathered around him. Together they all feasted and rejoiced. They brought him money and gold.

The Lord really blessed Job after his suffering. Indeed, He doubled Job's riches! Job soon owned twice as many animals–sheep, camels, oxen, donkeys. And that is not all. God gave Job seven more sons and three more daughters. Can you imagine how happy he and his wife were? Job praised and thanked God for His goodness. He loved the Lord and served Him more than ever.

Do you think Job's new family was curious about his past? I do. Let's try to imagine their questions and their father's answers. Could it have been like this? . . .

One son would have asked, "How did all your trouble begin? What were our brothers and sisters like? Please tell us how God spoke to you.

2. JOB'S NEW UNDERSTANDING ABOUT GOD

Show Illustration #14

Job would have answered, "My children, the Lord God is great. I cannot understand His power. (See Job 36:26.) He always existed. He created and controls everything–the earth, the sky, the sea. He–the God of Heaven and earth–created you and me. I do not understand how He did all this. But I know He did because He told me so. And I believe Him. (See Job 38:1-41.)

"Once my body was covered with sores. I thought then that God did not care about me. I felt He did not even see me. I sat on an ash heap like a beggar. I kept asking 'Why? Why? Why is this happening to me?' I thought God did not care about my suffering. I cannot tell you how my heart and body ached."

Their mother added, "I am ashamed to say I never encouraged him. I was too angry, too bitter to help your father. Your ten brothers and sisters were dead. All our animals and most of our servants were gone. So my heart was broken. And I cried a lot. I thought the Lord had really forgotten us. I was certain He did not care about us. I even encouraged your father to curse God. But he refused to do that."

Job added, "I often said, 'I wish I could see God. If only I could find Him. I wish He would speak to me face to face.' But I did not really think He would. "My friends had been criticizing me. They kept telling me I was a great sinner. They said my children were dead because of living sinfully. I was too discouraged to answer them. Then one day something marvelous happened.

"The Lord God spoke to me! Think of it! The Creator of all the universe talked to me! I was in the presence of the Almighty One. I couldn't speak. I was awed by His majesty. I heard God's voice with my own ears. I bowed humbly and listened to Him. The Lord asked me many questions. I will ask you, my children, some of the same questions. See if you can answer them," said Job.

"Do you understand how God keeps the seas in their boundaries?" The children shook their heads. "Do you know how God makes thunder and lightning? How does He make the rain and snow? Do you understand how wild animals give birth to their young? Do you understand how they feed? Do you understand how the birds fly? Do you know how to keep the stars in the sky? Can you count the stars?"

All agreed that these are great mysteries.

Job continued, "The Lord God performs all these wonders. They do not simply happen. God is far greater and much more powerful than man. I am nothing before Him." Softly Job added, "Yet God does not despise me. (See Job 36:5.) He watches over me all the time. (See Job 36:7.) He knows all about me. And He cares for me! I do not understand this. But I praise Him and thank Him."

This same powerful God loves you. He knows all that will ever happen to you. He sees you right now. Should this make a difference in the way you live? Should it make a difference in the places you go? In the things you say? Remember! The Lord knows all about you. He sees you at all times everywhere. And He is always with you in all places. (See Psalm 139:6-12.)

3. JOB'S NEW UNDERSTANDING ABOUT SUFFERING

Show Illustration #15

Job and his sons had much to talk about. One asked, "Why do you think God let you suffer? You had more suffering than anyone in our land."

"My son, I asked that same question over and over again. During those awful days, I often said, 'I am a good man. I am as good as anyone. I do not deserve all this dreadful suffering. I worship God. I obey Him. I help the poor.'

"I do not understand why God allowed those awful experiences. But certain matters are now clear to me:

1. "I know the Lord much better than before. Previously He had never spoken to me. While I was suffering, I heard His voice. He caused me to understand that He has all power. He showed me He is in control of everything–including me.

2. "Before my suffering, I thought I was a good man. Now I know I'm not worthy of God's blessings. All that He gives me–including suffering–is for my good. I don't deserve His goodness. There is nothing worthwhile in me. But the God of Heaven and earth loves me. He truly does.

3. "During that terrible time I thought the Lord had forgotten me. Now I know that He is faithful and never forsakes me.

4. "I began to understand the majesty and wisdom of God. Then I realized that He is perfectly righteous. He is never unjust, never evil. He always does what is right."

Another son asked Job, "Are Eliphaz, Bildad and Zophar really your friends?

Students, would you have considered them friends?

Listen to Job's answer. "Those three hurt me deeply. I was angry with them. It is never easy to love those who falsely accuse us," Job answered. "But the Lord showed me I must forgive them. He told them they were wrong. God said they had spoken falsely about Him. That was sin. He commanded them to offer sacrifices for their sin. And He forgave them.

"Then God commanded me to pray for them. And when I did, He made me well and prosperous again. Yes, those men are my friends today."

How should we treat those who are unkind to us? Is it hard to forgive them? Is it easy to be kind to them? Peter once asked the Lord, "How often shall my brother sin against me, and I forgive him? Till seven times?" Jesus said unto him, "I say not unto thee, Until seven times: but, Until 70 times seven." (See Matthew 18:21-22.) This is the teaching of the Lord Jesus Christ.

Job did not understand why so much evil happened to him. But he did know this: Everything works together for good to those who love God (Romans 8:28).

4. LESSONS LEARNED FROM JOB

What have you learned from the testing of Job? (Let students discuss.) Have you ever suffered? Will you tell us what lessons you learned from your trial? (Encourage response.)

We have been memorizing a wonderful Bible verse. Let's quote James 1:12 together. Did Job love God? *(Indeed, he did.)* Was he tested? *(Oh, yes!)* According to James 1:12, what will Job receive some day?

Show Illustration #16

Job will receive a crown of life–a reward for suffering. But he never knew this! Why? Because he lived hundreds of years before God revealed this truth.

Someday, all who trust in the Lord will stand before Him. (Read Romans 14:10; 1 Corinthians 3:12-15; 2 Corinthians 5:10.) Each will receive any rewards he may have earned. As long as we are on earth, Christian believers will have testings. Some will suffer physically, as did Job.

Others will suffer the pain of discipline. (Read Hebrews 12:5-7 slowly.) Did your father ever discipline you? Why? Did that mean he did not love you? No, he wanted you to be obedient. God, our heavenly Father, wants us to obey Him. If we are disobedient, he may cause us to suffer. Maybe we ignore Him. Perhaps we do not bother to read the Bible or pray. If so, the Lord may use trials to get our attention.

At times, we may be thinking only of ourselves. Instead, we should keep looking to the Lord Jesus. (Read Hebrews 12:2a.) Remember how Elihu reminded Job to think about God, not himself? Self-thinking may result in receiving testing from the Lord.

God often allows trials to make us stronger Christians. (Read Job 23:10; James 1:3-4.) Like Job, we are purified by testings.

The Lord may send suffering as punishment for sin. But He promises forgiveness when we confess our sin. (Read Proverbs 28:13; 1 John 1:9.)

At this moment our enemy, the devil, is busy. Like a roaring lion, he is seeking whom he may devour. (See 1 Peter 5:8-9.) He is striving to keep unbelievers from receiving Christ as Saviour. If you belong to the Lord, Satan wants you to dishonor Him. He tries to get you to laugh at God and His Son.

You must resist the devil. And God's Holy Spirit wants to help you do this. You have to come close to God by reading His Word. (See James 4:7-8.) With His Word in your heart, you know how to avoid sin. (See Psalm 119:9, 11.) And you must pray to be kept from sinning. (See Ephesians 6:10-11, 17-18.)

When you trust is in the Saviour, He lives within you. And remember: He is stronger than the devil (1 John 4:4). The Lord Jesus can give you power to say "no" to Satan.

God will never allow His own to be tested too much. He will say to the devil, "That is enough." He did this for Job. He will do it for you. (Read 1 Corinthians 10:13.)

You can be certain of this: The Lord will allow trials in your life. Job could say, "When God has tried me, I shall come forth as gold" (Job 23:10). In his trial, Job said, "God is performing what He has planned for me" (Job 23:14.) The Lord loved Job so much that He did what was best for him. And He will do what is best for you. (Read Romans 8:28.) Do you believe this? Will you thank the Lord that it is so?

If possible, have your group sing, *How Great Thou Art*.

www.ingramcontent.com/pod-product-compliance
Lightning Source LLC
Chambersburg PA
CBHW060801090426
42736CB00002B/116